Let's explore Dub

Gurkiran Sandhu

One day, I was reading about the tallest buildings in the world and I read about Burj Khalifa in Dubai. At that moment, I decided I wanted to visit Dubai.

When I landed in Dubai, the first thing I did was to take the Dubai Metro rail to the gorgeous Dubai Mall.

Dubai Mall is grand, huge and contains beautiful structures along with many shops. I was extremely fascinated by a structure showing many men diving in the water as it created a very soothing effect.

In addition, the mall also contains a very large and mesmerizing aquarium with is absolutely a delight a see. It gives you an opportunity to explore different kinds of fish and sea creatures swimming in the beautiful blue water.

In the mall, there is a huge food court available that offers many different kinds of restaurants.

I wanted to try some authentic Arabic food and had some delicious shish kebabs at a traditional restaurant named Burj Al Hamam. Shish kebab is a dish of skewered and grilled cubes of meat.

In the evening, I stepped out of the mall and saw the tallest building in the world, Burj Khalifa.

Did you know?

1. Burj Khalifa has the longest single running elevator, which is 140 floors. The elevators go 10 meters per second and are among the fastest in the world.

2. The tip of the sphere of the Burj Khalifa can be seen up to 95 kilometers away.

3. Burj Khalifa has the highest number of stories in the world.

After admiring the beauty and grace of the tall Burj Khalifa, I enjoyed the water fountain show right outside of Burj Khalifa.

Did you know?

1. The Dubai Fountain is the world's largest choreographed fountain system set on the 30-acre manmade Burj Khalifa Lake.

2. It is illuminated by 6,600 lights and 25 colored projectors, it is 275 meters long and shoots water up to 500 feet.

3. The fountain is choreographed using the sounds of classical Arabic music.

The next morning, I took a Taxi to go to Burj Al Arab – the luxury hotel in Dubai.

Did you know?

1. Burj Al Arab is the fourth tallest hotel in the world.

2. It stands on an artificial island 280 meters from Jumeirah beach and is connected to the mainland by a private curving bridge.

3. The shape of the structure is designed to mimic the sail of a ship and it has a helipad near the roof at a height of 210 meters above ground.

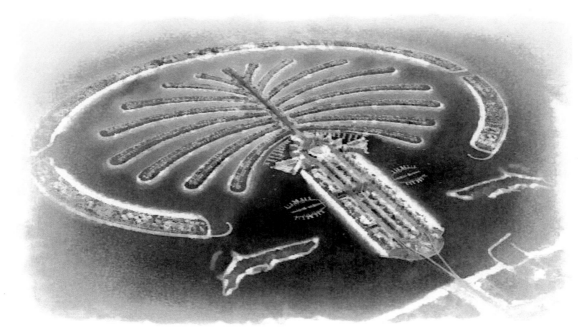

A few miles away from Burj Al Arab is the very beautiful Palm Jumeirah. Palm Jumeirah is an artificial group of islands with numerous hotels and dining destinations.

The Atlantis Hotel in Dubai is one of the hotels in Palm Jumeriah. It was the first resort to be built on the island and is themed on the myth of Atlantis, but includes distinct Arabian elements.

In the evening, I enjoyed a traditional Arabic performance of a Belly dancer who elegantly danced on the amazing tunes of Arabic music and then, I went back to my hotel room to get some rest.

The next morning, I took a morning desert safari which was one of the best experiences of my life!

I enjoyed a camel ride as we took the tour of the desert and in the afternoon, I tried a traditional Arabic drink called "Tamar Hindi".

Tamar Hindi is a drink made by combining soaked, crushed tamarind with water, sugar and lemon juice. Tamar Hindi is perfectly sweet with a tangy kick, and was traditionally served across the Levant by travelling peddlers.

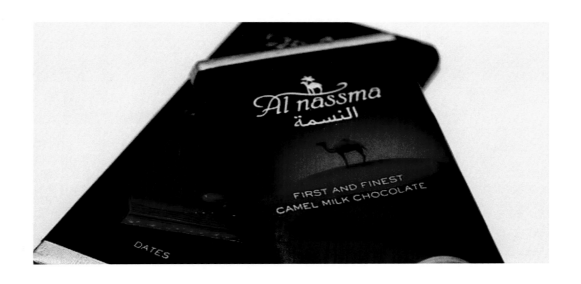

In the evening, I visited a shop near my hotel and tasted a chocolate made from Camel milk. It was a very interesting and a unique experience because I had never tried camel milk before.

As a souvenir, I decided to take some currency of Dubai back home. The currency of Dubai is called 'Dirham'.

After having such a great time in Dubai and to complete my Arabic experience, I took my flight back home using Emirates Airlines. Emirates is an airline based in Dubai, United Arab Emirates and is considered one of the most luxurious airlines in the world.

Look for other interesting Travel Books on Amazon.com

Let's explore Australia, Kids!

Gurkiran Sandhu

Let's explore India, Kids!

Gurkiran Sandhu

Let's explore Switzerland, Kids!

Gurkiran Sandhu

Let's Explore China, Kids!

Gurkiran Sandhu

Let's explore Dubai, Kids!
Gurkiran Sandhu

Made in the USA
San Bernardino, CA
22 July 2018